guitar
note
finder

GUITAR NOTE FINDER
by Ashkan Mashhour

ISBN: 978-1-939619-05-1
COVER & INTERIOR DESIGN, TYPESETTING, MUSIC ENGRAVING,
ARTWORK, PREPRESS: Ashkan Mashhour

For inquiries, feedback, and suggestions, please contact:
ashkan@cheatsheetmusic.com
For updates and the latest information, visit:
pelemeleworks.com

pelemeleworks.com

contents

guitarnotefinder

The purpose of this book is to **learn the names of the notes** on the fretboard,[1] to **recognise them immediately**, and to **associate them to a note on the music staff**, and vice versa.

There are many ways to go about learning the fretboard: notes on each string, notes on the same fret across strings, scales, counting frets from the open string, octaves, 5th/10th/12th frets, etc. Such mnemonic devices help *find your way* but they are an extra step. They take a moment longer than an instant, simply because you have to relate the note to something else first! Here, the focus is on visualising one note at a time. Seeing each note in isolation, where it sits on the fretboard, and conjointly where it sits on the music staff, will foster immediate recognition. This will help *know your way* around the fretboard.

Learning the notes on the fretboard is a memorisation effort: 78 notes over 12 frets across 6 strings. To commit note names to memory, divide and repeat, before you conquer. Give it time, don't expect to memorise the entire fretboard in a week. A few steps will help you minimise this effort while keeping the goal in mind: name notes on the neck in a flash. The direct relationship between one fretboard location and one note must be **hardwired** in your head! This book is for standard tuning E A D G B E.

1. Break up the fretboard into three sections: Frets 0–4, Frets 5–8, and Frets 9–12. Each section is a position wide (four frets or so).
2. Memorise natural notes in each section. Sharp/flat notes will come as a by-product: one fret up (♯) or one fret down (♭) the string. You can limit yourself to memorising one string at a time, in any given section (that's only two to three natural notes).
3. If reading music or sight-reading matters to you (it should!), map each note on the fretboard to its corresponding pitch on the music staff, and back.
4. Give yourself a break with these safety nets. Recognise that the low E string and the high E string feature the same note names, like-for-like. The order of notes on a string is always that of the musical alphabet (**A--B-C--D--E-F--G**--A), repeating every 12 frets. Remember that notes B & C and E & F are always next to each other on the same string. And use the fretboard markers as visual landmarks.
5. Drill this knowledge in by working through the quiz (question–answer) in the following pages.
6. Once you gain some proficiency with note location, time yourself. Tap with your foot or bring on the metronome. Set the tempo to 40 bpm or lower. Start slowly to recognise one note anywhere on the first 12 frets (go through the quiz). Ultimately, identifying a note on the fretboard shouldn't take more than a fraction of a second.

---

1. The fretboard is also called the *fingerboard* or the *neck*.

The first part of this book presents all necessary reference charts. The second part is a quiz and presents two neck diagrams on a page and the corresponding music staves on the following page, within a section of the fretboard. The quiz is organised in three sections: Frets 0–4, Frets 5–8, Frets 9–12. Notes on a same page are all mixed up within that section and unrelated to one another. Here are possible usage examples.

- **Note on fretboard ➡ note name / note on music staff.** Look at the page showing a note on the fretboard. What is the note name? Where does it lie on the music staff? Turn the page over and check your answers. For a sharp or flat note (e.g. F♯ or G♭), either is shown on the staff but both are correct answers (*enharmonic* equivalents).
- **Note name / note on music staff ➡ note on fretboard.** Look at the page showing a note on the music staff. Where does it lie on the fretboard? Flip back to the previous page and check your answer.

You can go through the three sections of the quiz in sequence or open a page at random each time. Spend a good amount of time on each section before moving to the next, even if not fully mastered. Take a breather and return to that section after a while—it will allow you to digest the information, while you're working on a different section.

Alternatively, with the metronome set on a slow dial (e.g. 40 bpm), go through an entire section or all three sections without stopping. Write down your answers for each page on blank music staff or neck diagram paper. Then go back and check your answers.

Any of these methods works with or without the guitar, either playing each note on the instrument, picturing your answers in your mind, naming them aloud, or writing them down on blank music paper. You can concentrate on learning the note on the fretboard and its name first, and leave the pitch information on the staff for later. If you choose to use your guitar, fingering is free-form. Use the same finger throughout or allocate one finger per fret starting with the index finger (*position playing*). Frets 0–4, Frets 5–8, Frets 9–12 could be played in the first, fifth, and ninth position respectively (e.g. on Frets 5–8, play in 5th position with the index on fret 5, middle on 6, ring on 7, and pinkie on 8).

A peculiarity of the guitar is that the same pitch can be played at various locations on the fretboard (also referred to as *unison*). Be aware of this choice and don't confuse these same-pitch notes with the same note, octaves apart.

Octave patterns help you locate the same note octaves apart, strings and frets across. These patterns repeat all over the fretboard. Learn the patterns but for now, stash them away as the focus in this book, in learning the note names, is on seeing notes in isolation.

Example of a 7-day routine for each fretboard section:

Day 1: Learn (natural) note names on string 6, and corresponding music staff notation, for that section.

Day 2: Learn note names on string 5. Review notes on string 6.

Day 3: Learn note names on string 4. Review notes on strings 6–5.

Day 4: Learn note names on string 3. Review notes on strings 6–4.

Day 5: Learn note names on string 2. Review notes on strings 6–3.

Day 6: Learn note names on string 1. Review notes on strings 6–2.

Day 7: Review all strings. Take the quiz for that section. How are you doing?

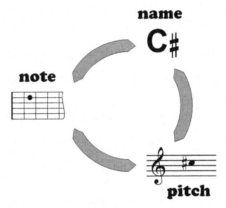

For additional information on the book and any updates, please visit: www.pelemeleworks.com

The following are tips and exercises you can think up to challenge yourself naming notes on the fretboard. They also underline some common weaker spots as one memorises the fretboard.

- Generally speaking, there is a tendency to learn the fretboard horizontally (along the neck or along a string), string by string. As an exercise, practise naming notes on the same fret across all six strings.

- Take some chords you know, finger them on the guitar, and name the notes (don't worry about enharmonic spellings). This will exercise vertical note naming, across all six strings.

- As you make progress in learning the notes on the neck and to shake things up, fragment the fretboard into other sections (four frets wide or larger) than those used in this book and go through a section naming the notes. For example, split the fretboard into frets 1–4, frets 4–7, frets 7–10, frets 10–13.

- On separate blank chord diagrams or neck diagrams, write down all occurrences of these four groups of notes: B & C; E & F; G & A; D. Focus on each group and you have the fretboard covered.

- Take two strings (e.g. 6 & 5). Set the metronome to 40–60 bpm. Cycle through the musical alphabet (A--B-C--D--E-F--G), playing one note per string on each beat, in this order, on frets 0–11. Switch strings on each beat. Say each note out loud. Variations: choose another pair of strings, choose three strings, include sharps/flats, etc.

- At your own pace, play random notes of the C major scale, targeting all 7 natural notes. Then play F♯ major pentatonic, targeting all 5 sharp/flat notes. Name each note internally and don't mindlessly follow a scale pattern. Limit yourself to a section of the fretboard (4–6 frets wide) or the first 12 frets.

- Don't neglect the 12th fret and above. The fretboard repeats its layout of frets 0–11 but it looks and feels different as all frets are much closer to one another. Fret 12 is the same as fret 0, one octave higher.

- Open string notes (EADGBE), notes on the 5th fret, and notes on the 10th fret are all natural notes. Notes on the 11th fret are all sharps/flats. Remember this but don't rely on it as an intermediate step.

- You learn to associate a fretboard location with its note name. Go the extra mile and also associate its pitch on the music staff. It takes little extra effort.

- Classical guitar methods offer progressive material organised in similar sections of the fretboard. They will further engrain note name and note position in your mind, with a side benefit of improving your sight-reading. Consider studying out of a few.

- There are 78 notes on the first 12 frets (+ open strings). Amongst those, there are 48 natural notes. Make it a goal to know the names of all 48 notes and their position on the music staff—independently and without any intermediary step. The goal is not to "work out notes"!

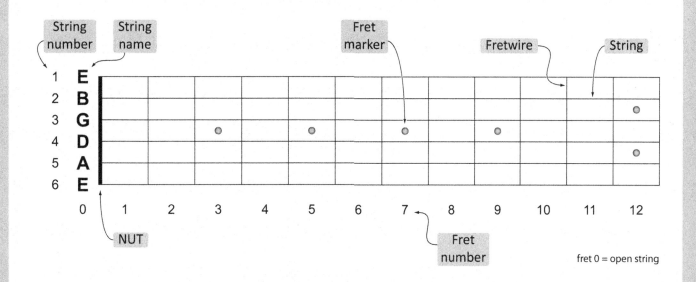

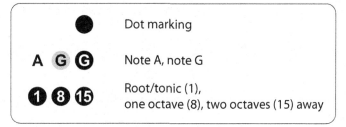

— half step (1 fret)
– – whole step (2 frets)

4th 4th 4th
4th 3rd

E A D G B E

1/2 step

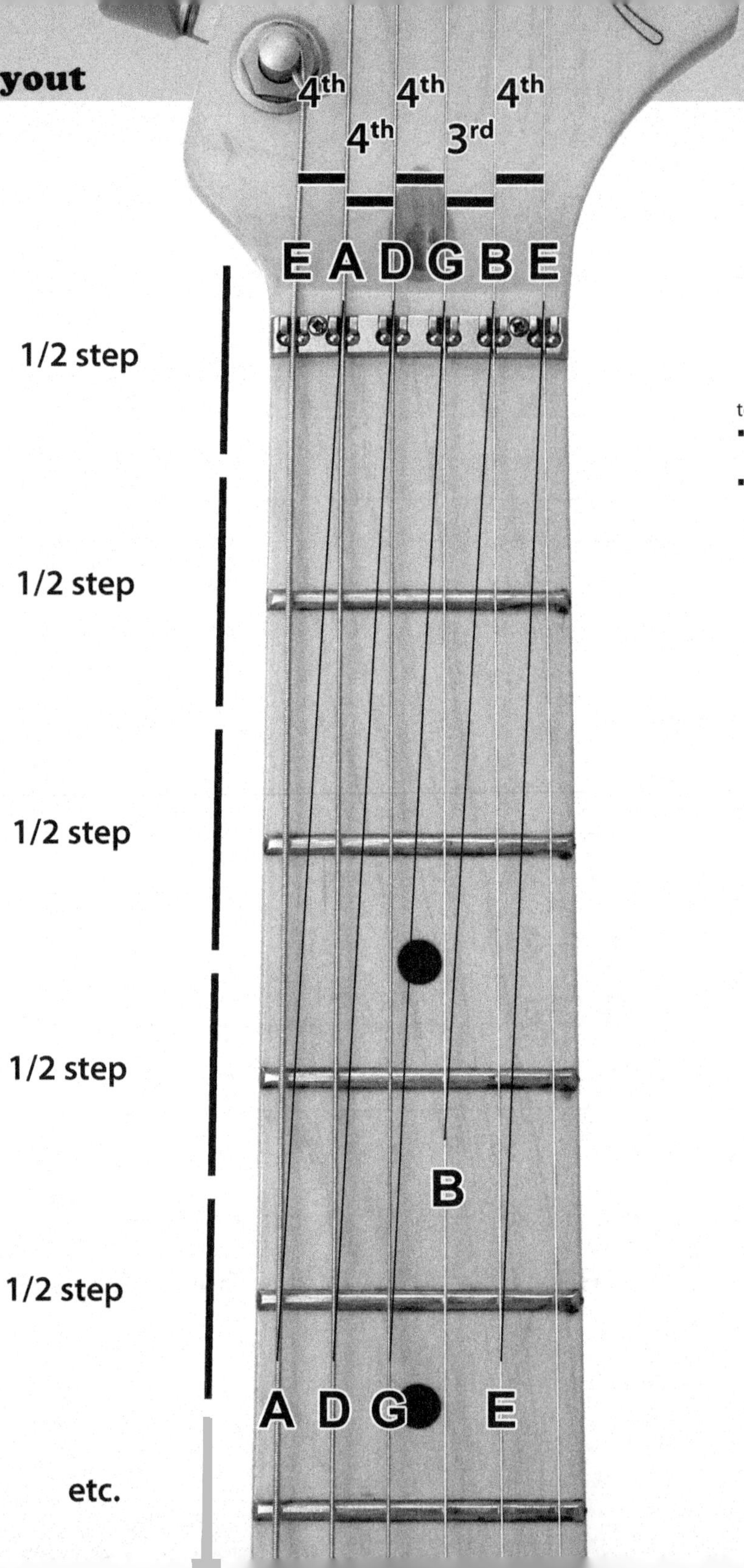

tonal distance (interval):
- between frets:
  half step
- between strings:
  perfect 4th
  strings 3 & 2, major 3rd

1/2 step

1/2 step

1/2 step

B

1/2 step

A D G E

etc.

guitarnotefinder

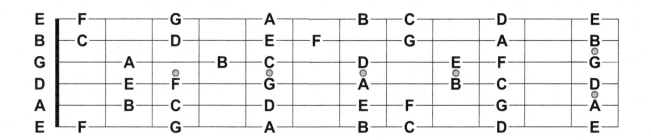

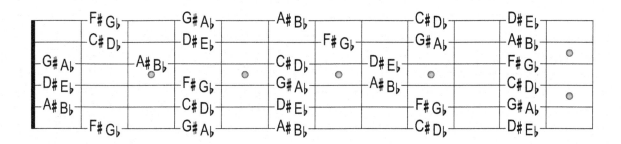

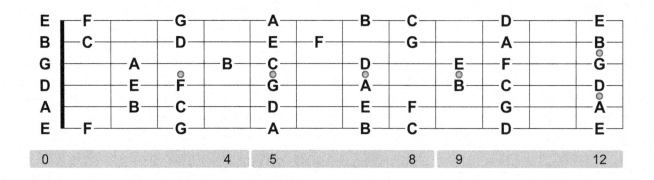

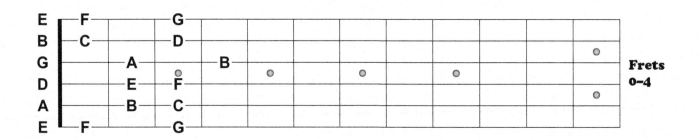

Frets
0–4

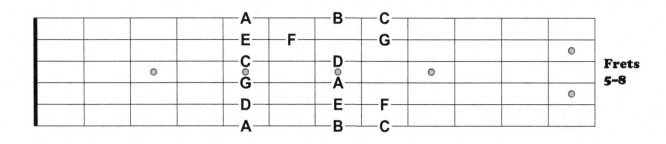

Frets
5–8

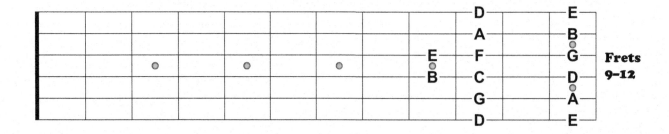

Frets
9–12

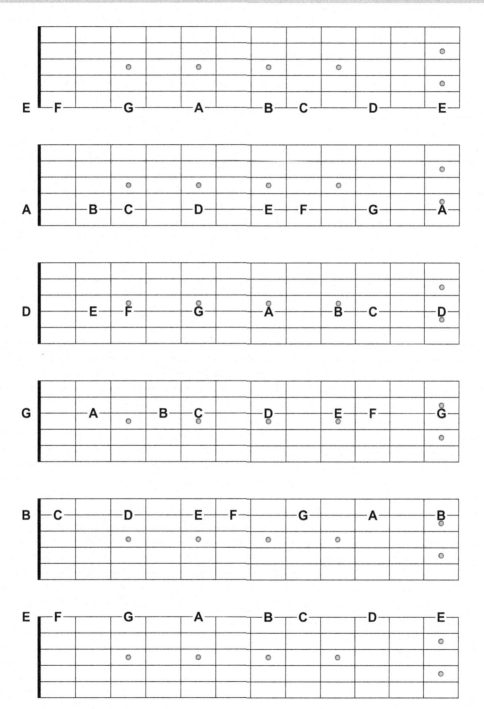

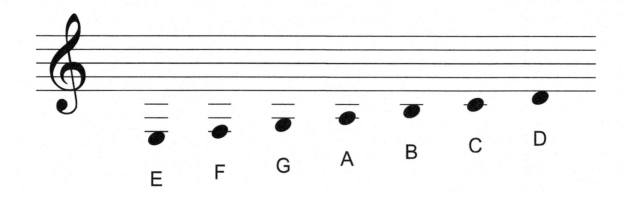

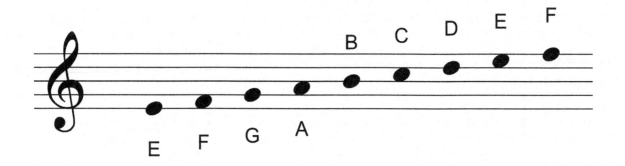

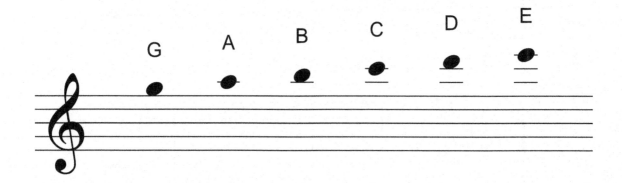

guitarnotefinder

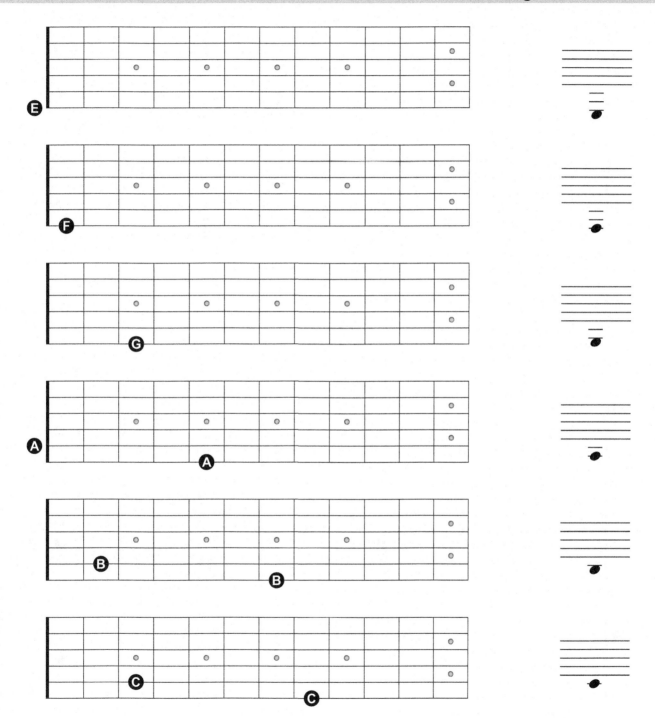

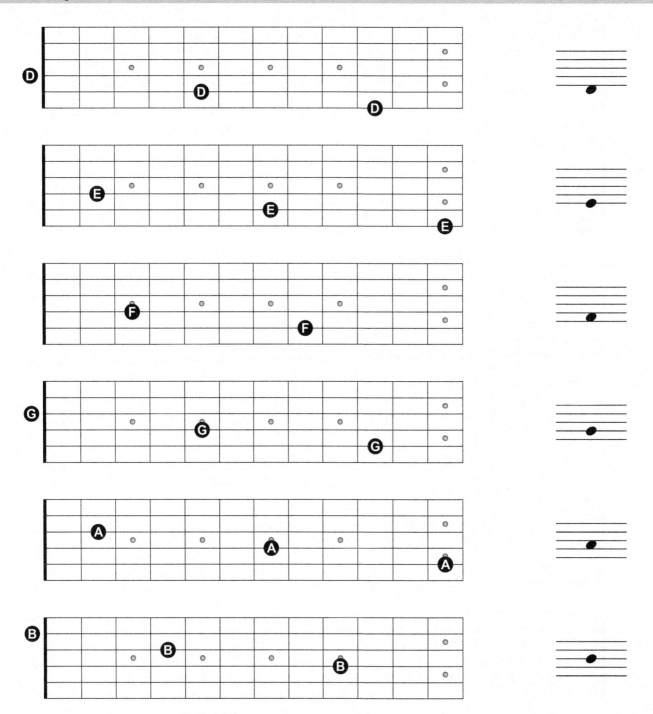

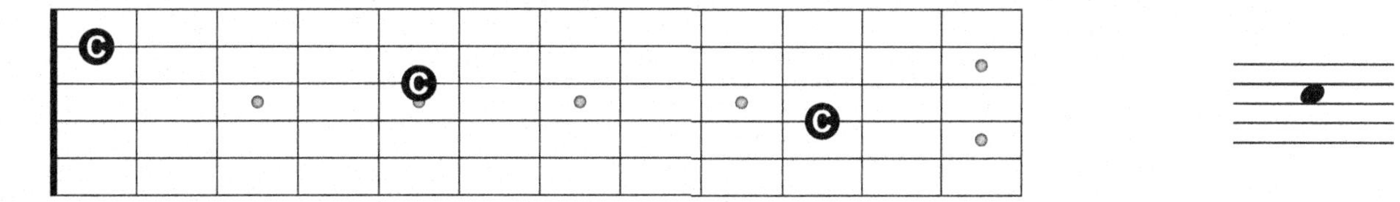
C
C
C

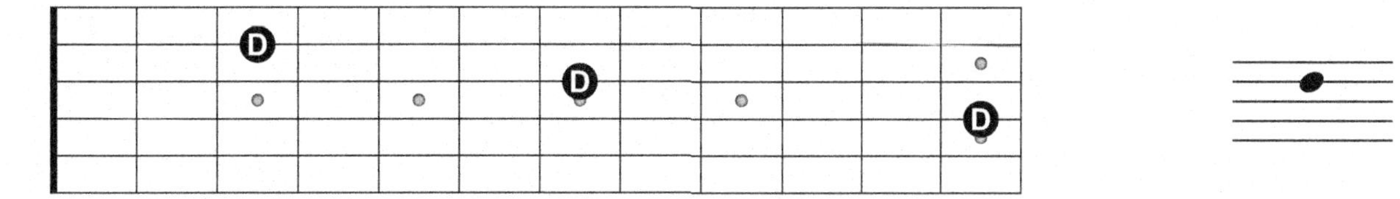
D
D
D

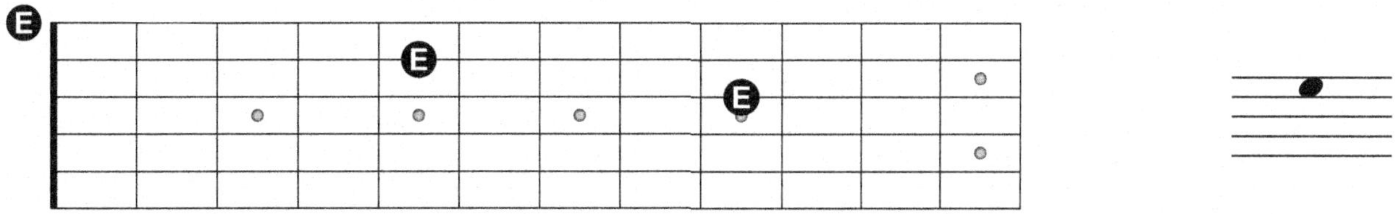
E
E
E

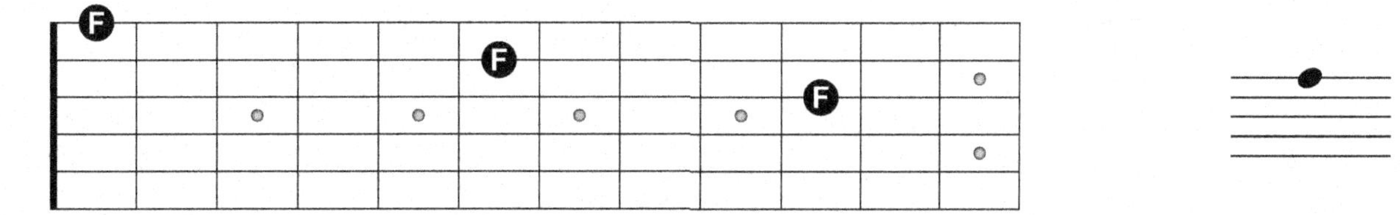
F
F
F

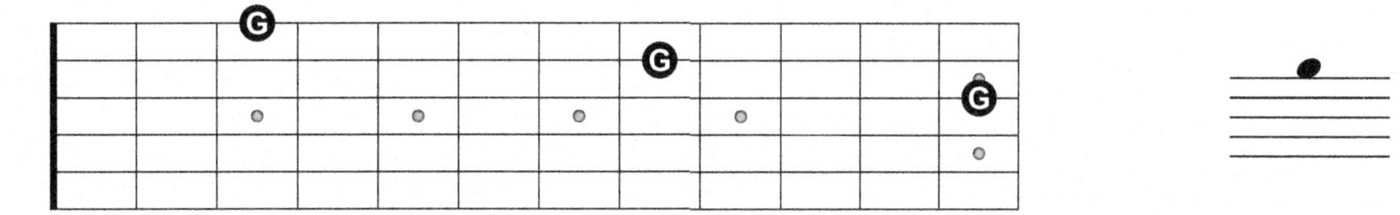
G
G
G

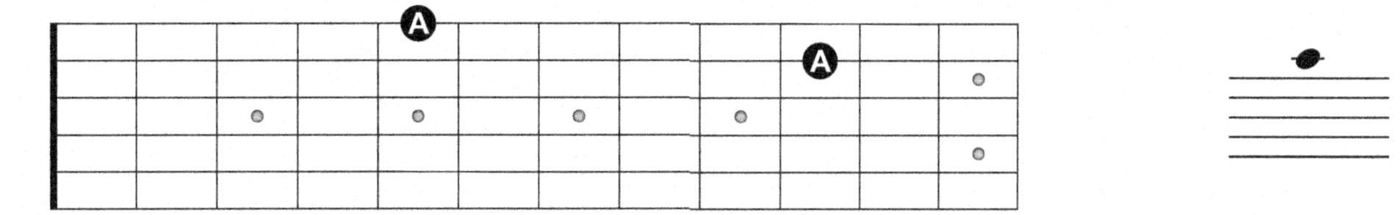
A
A

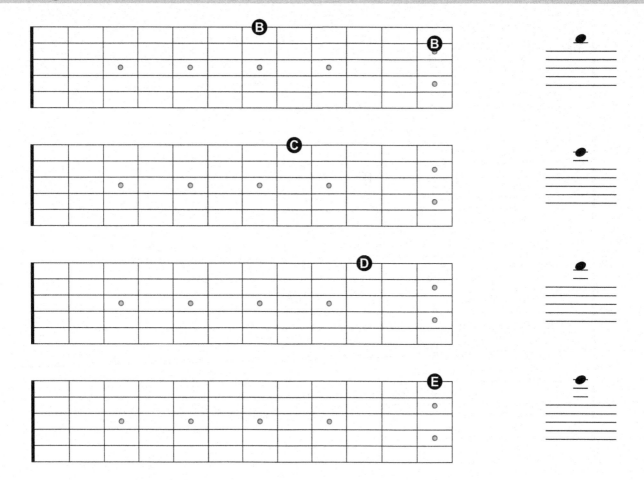

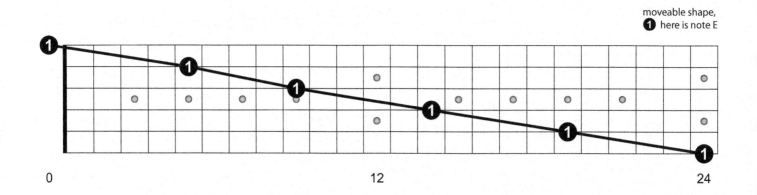

moveable shape,
1 here is note E

0   12   24

moveable shapes

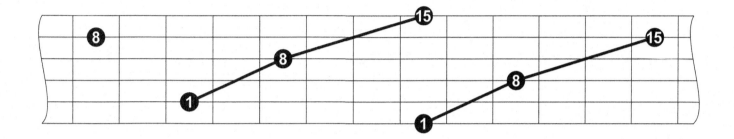

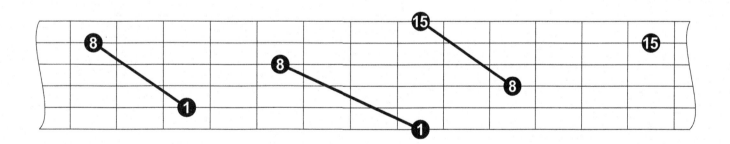

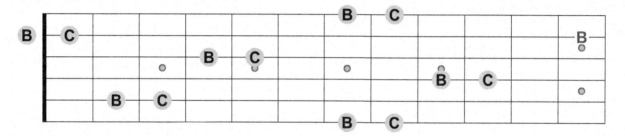

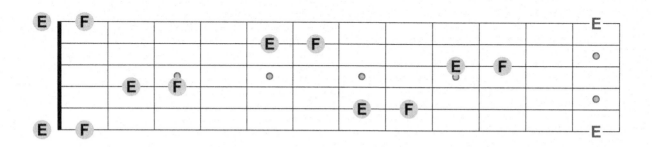

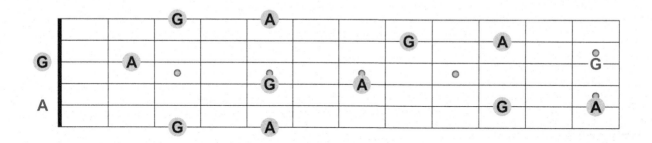

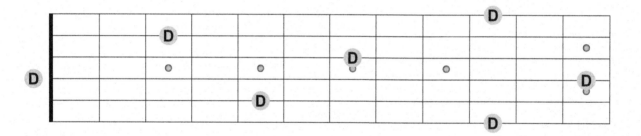

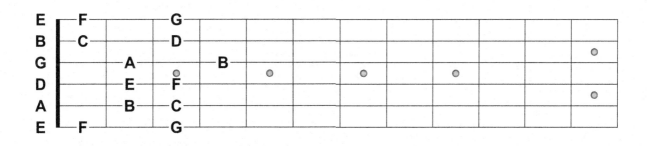

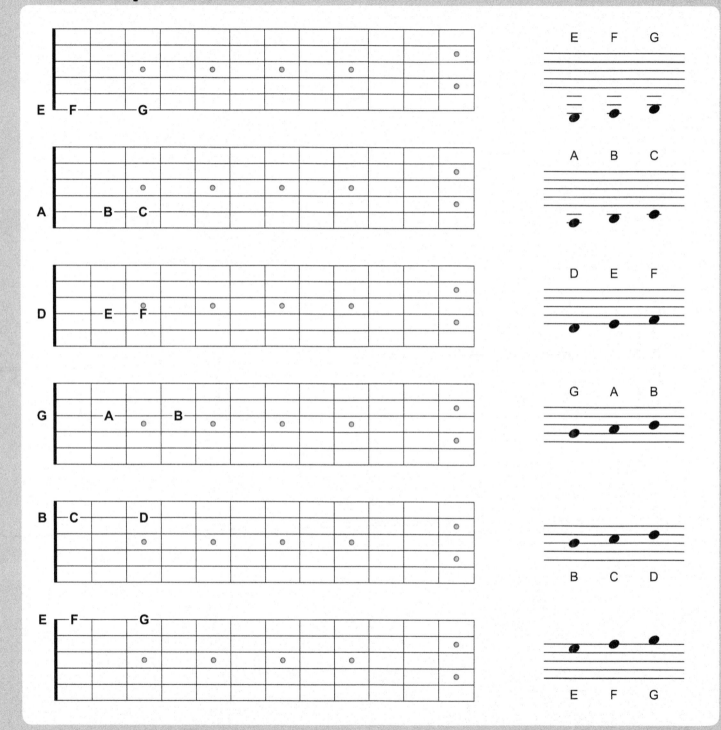

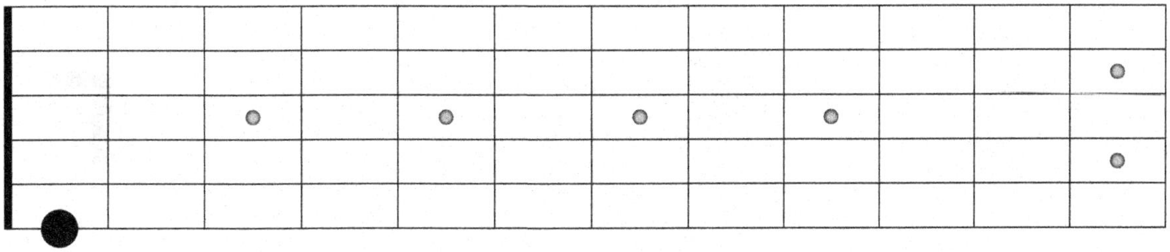

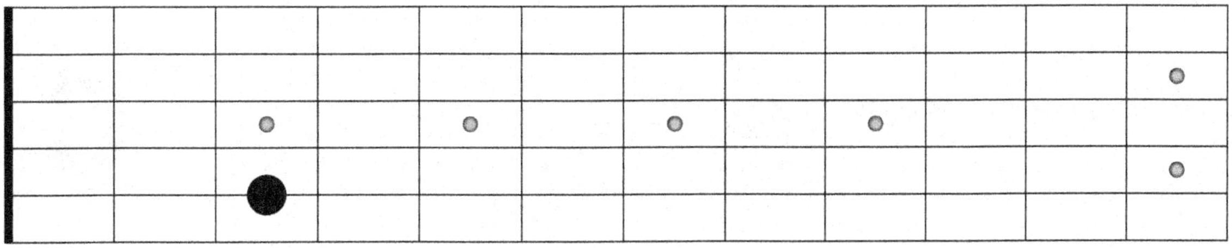

F

C

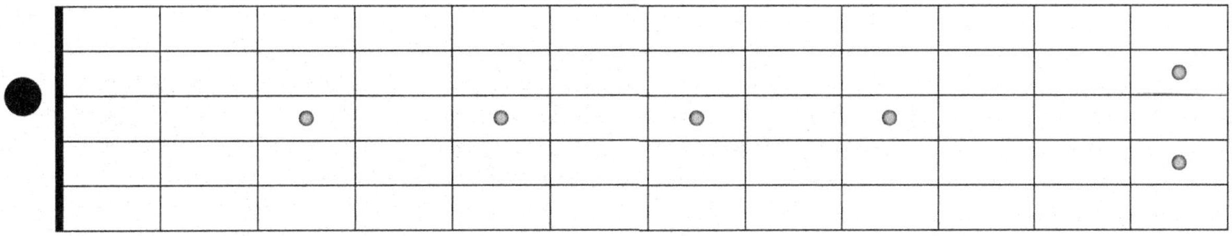

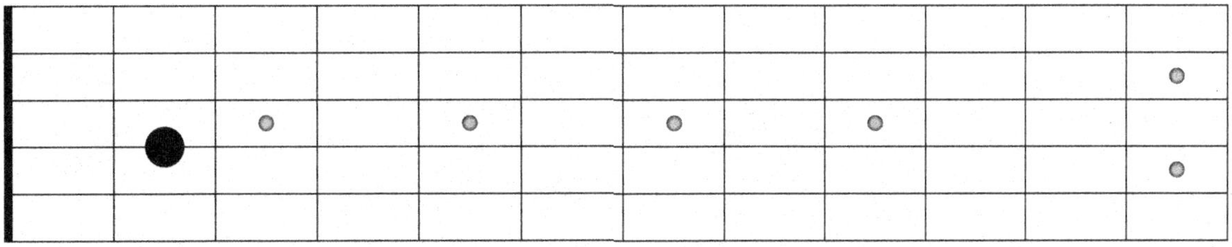

G

E

 **C#**

 **G♭**

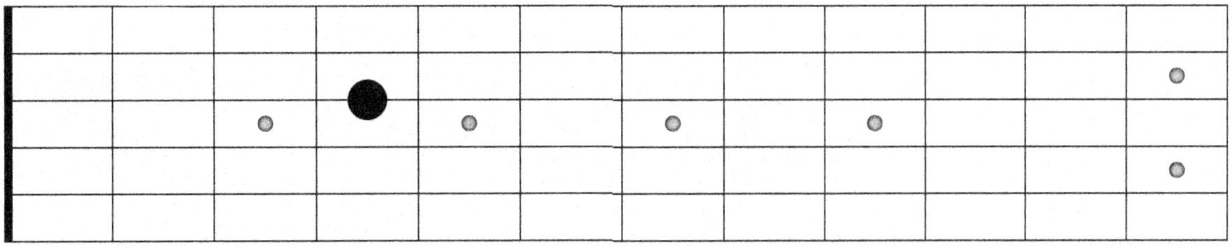

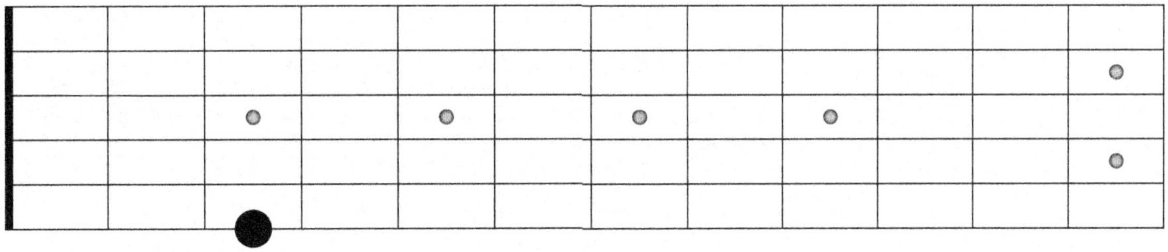

B

G

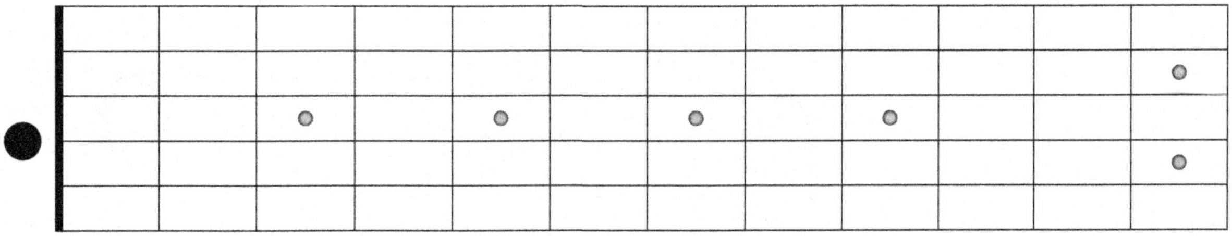

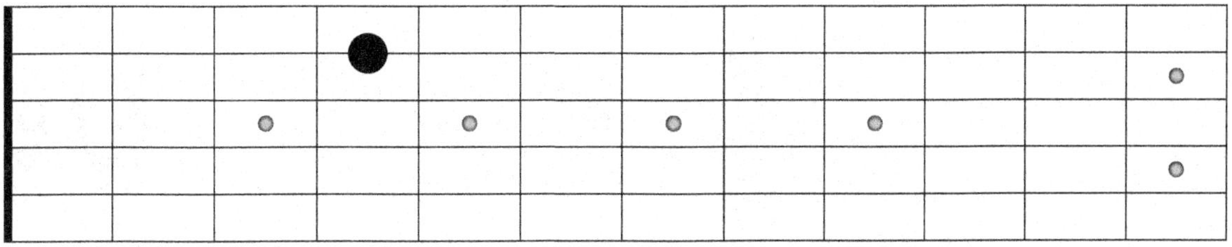

D

D#

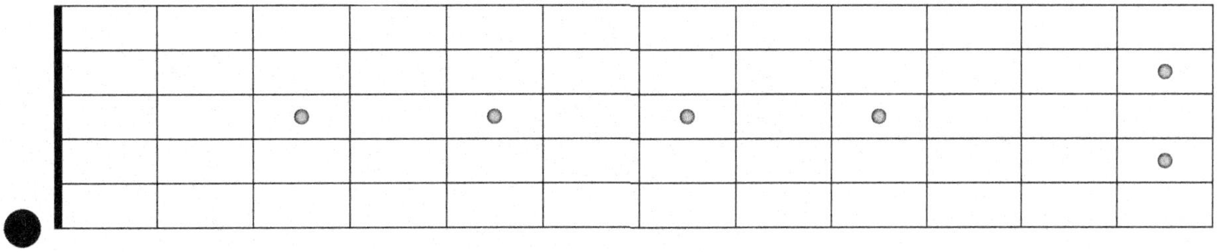

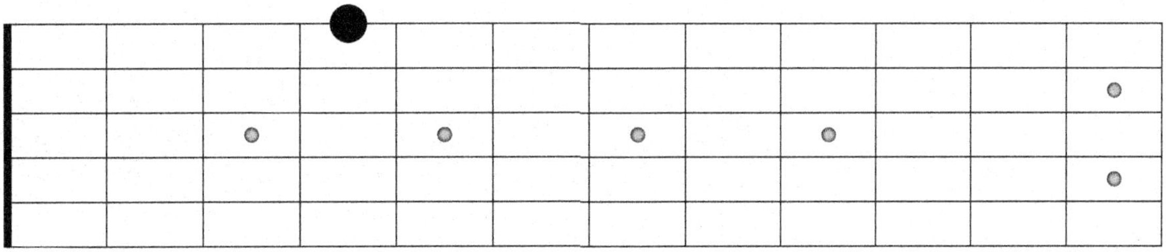

E

G#

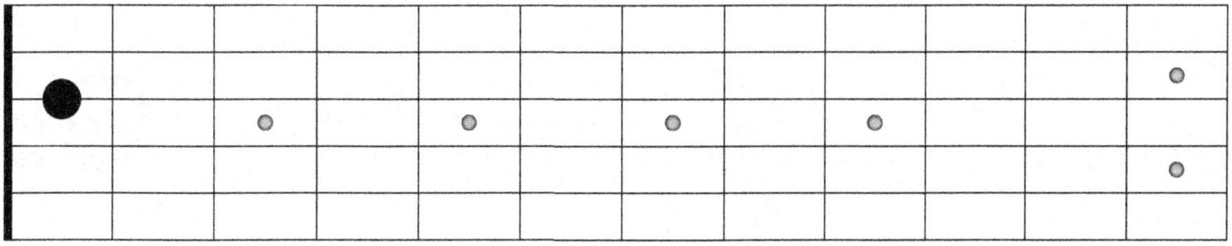

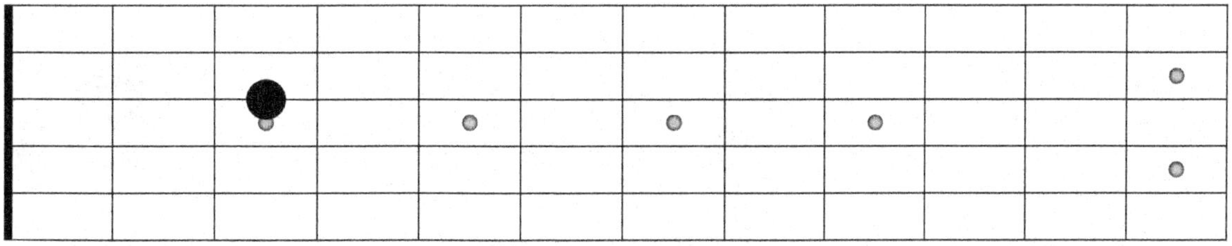

G#

B♭

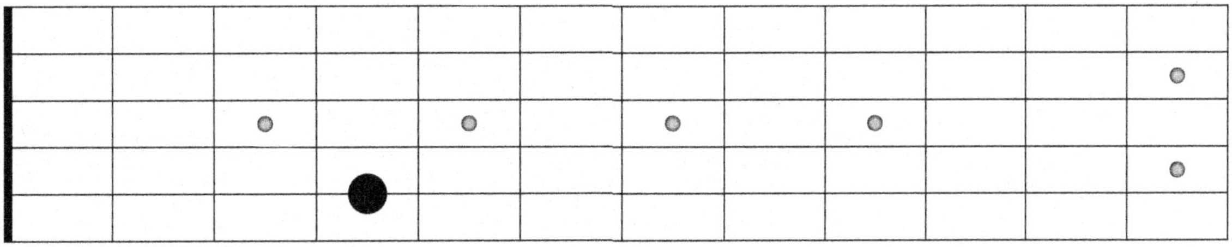

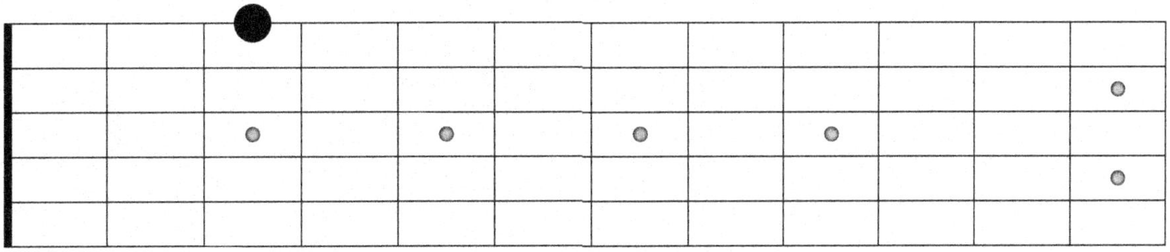

C♯

G

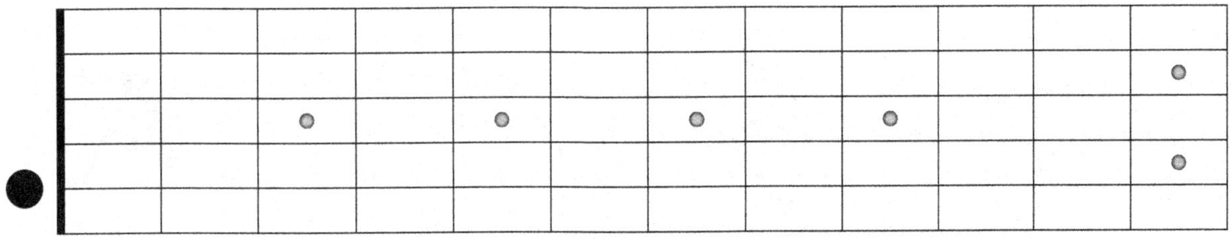

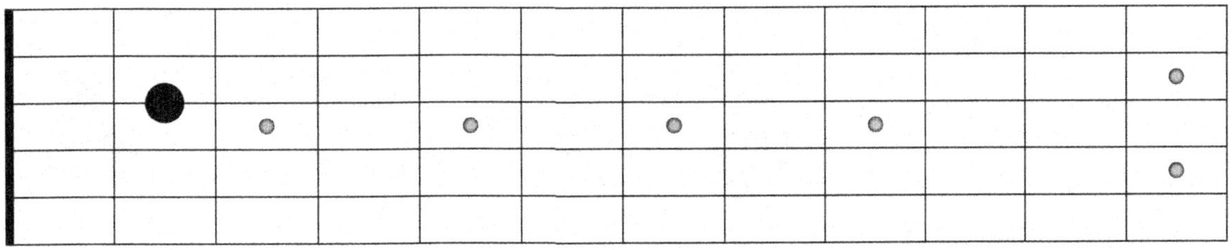

A

A

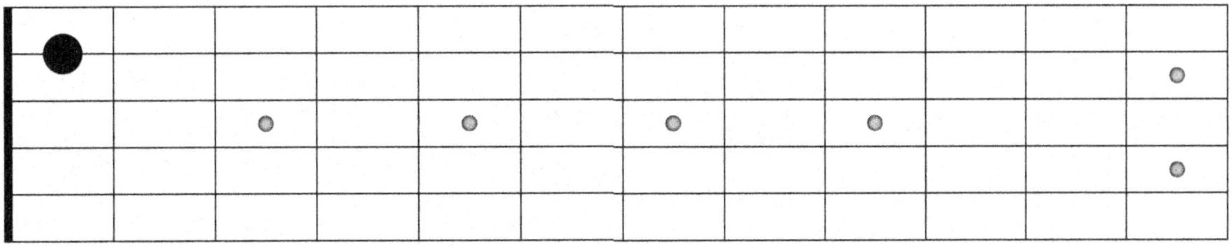

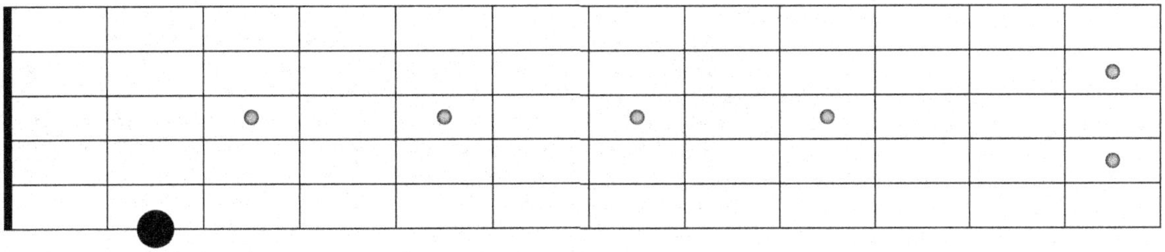

C

F#

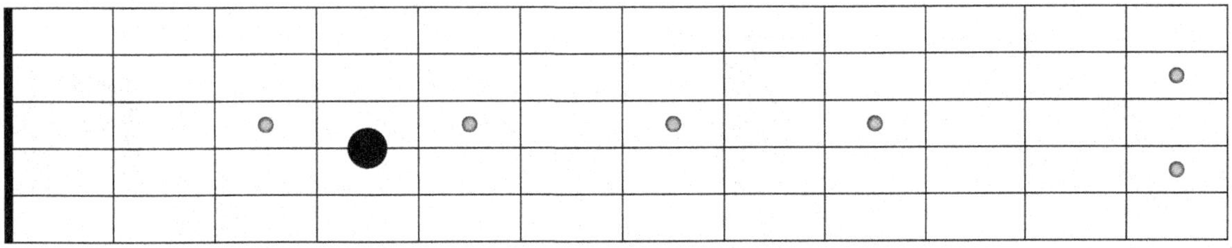

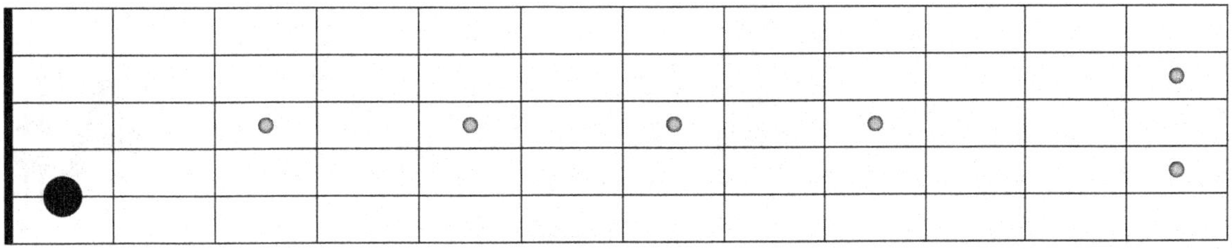

F#

A#

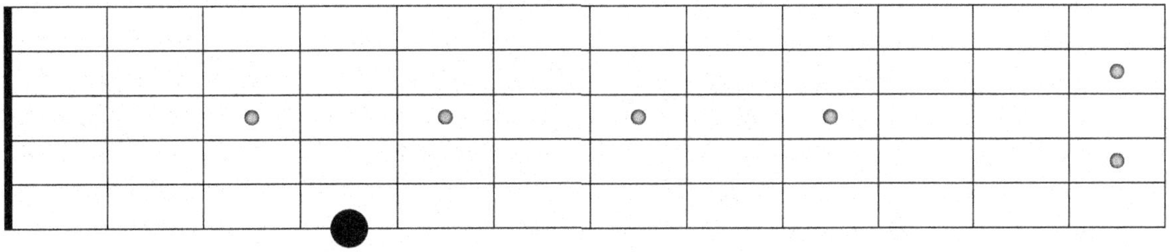

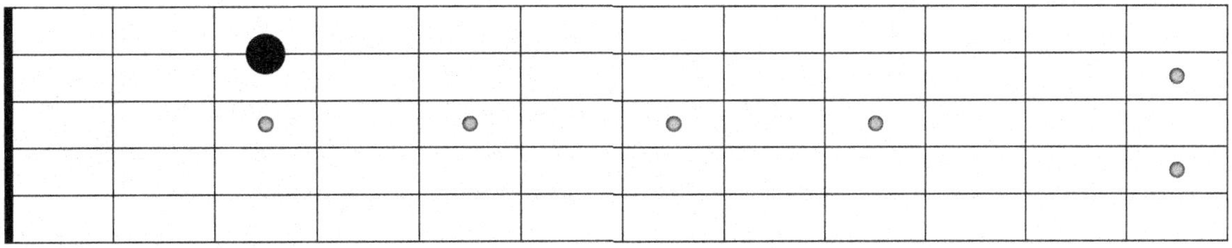

D

E

B

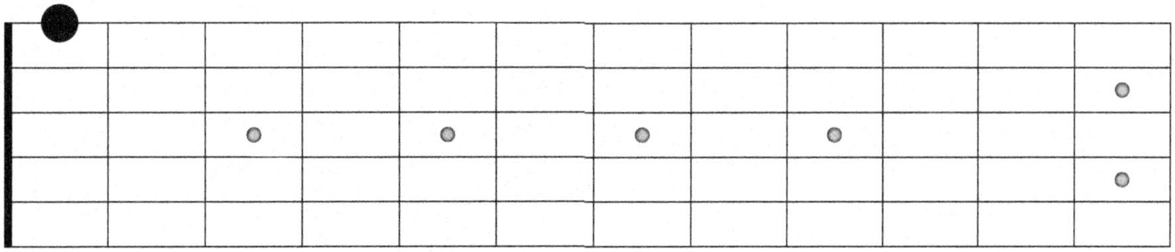

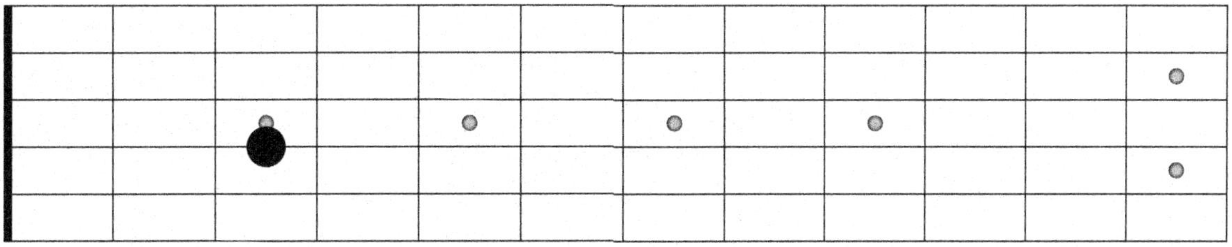

F

F

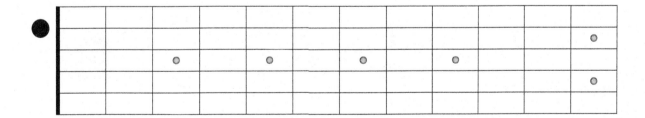

B

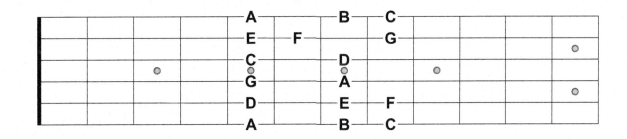

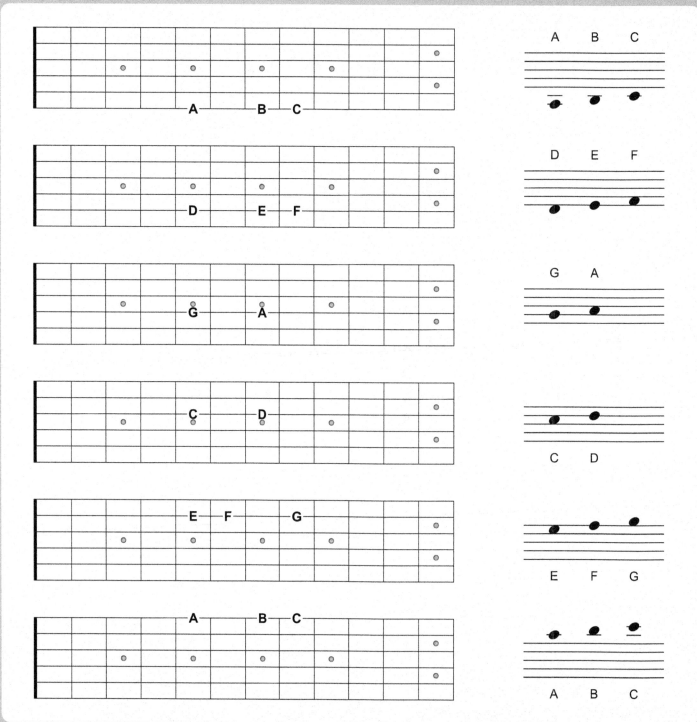

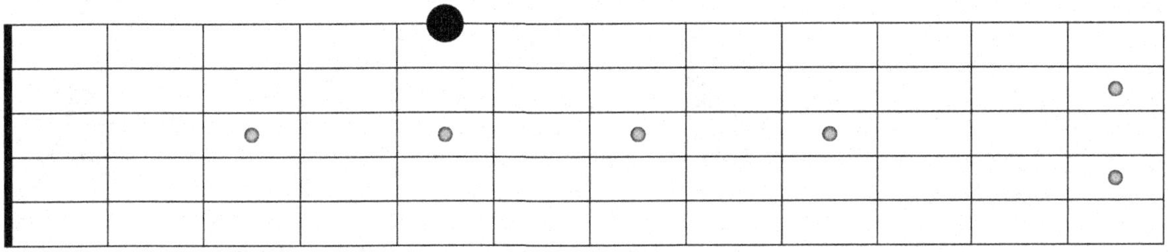

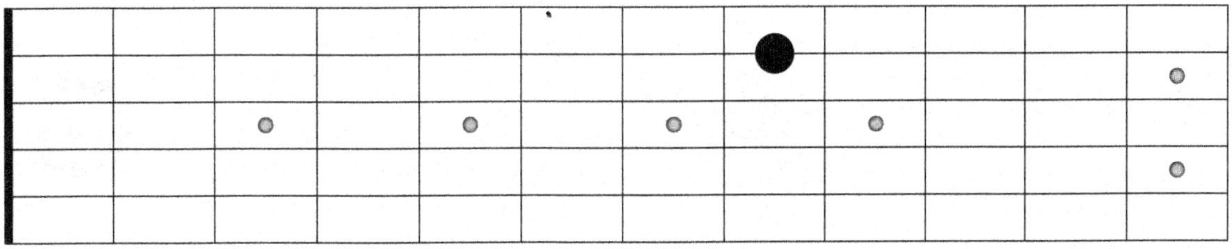

A

G

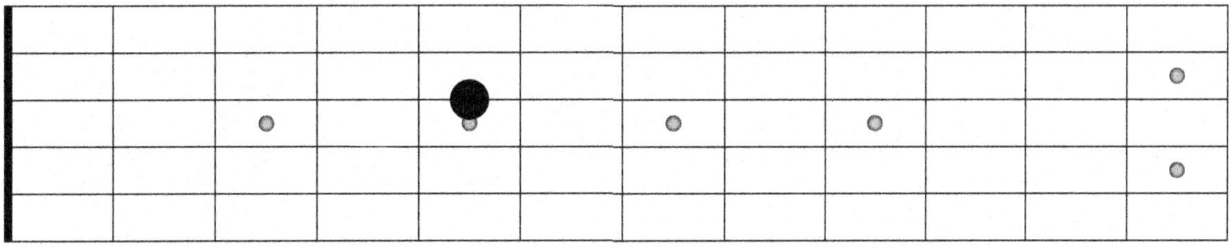

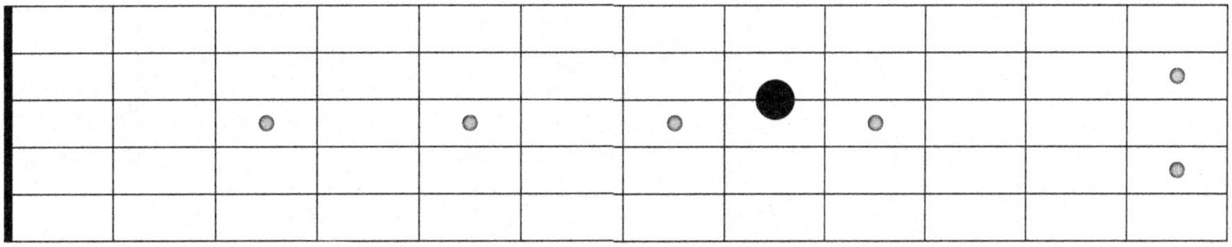

C

E♭

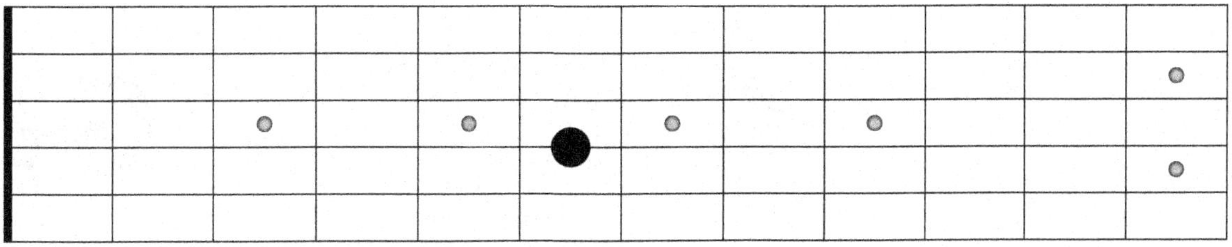

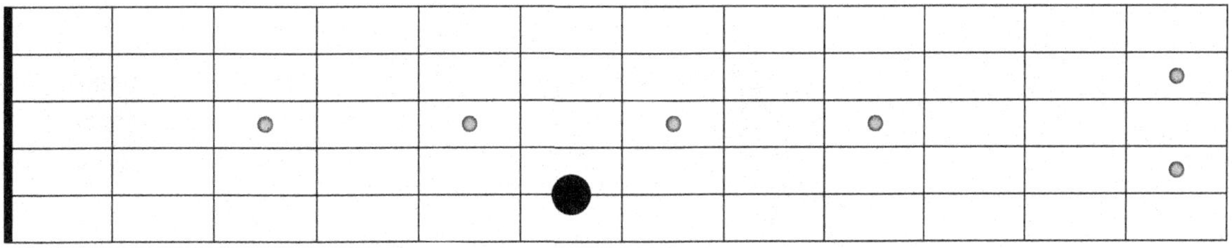

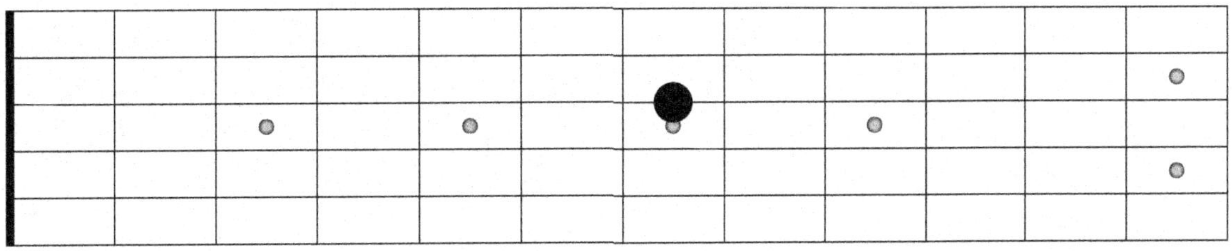

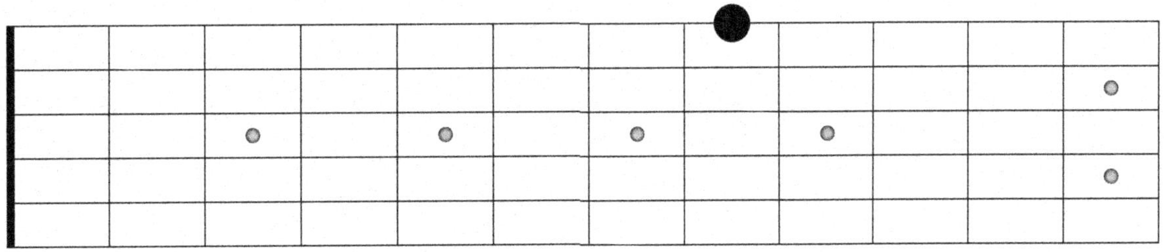

D

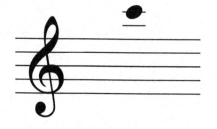

C

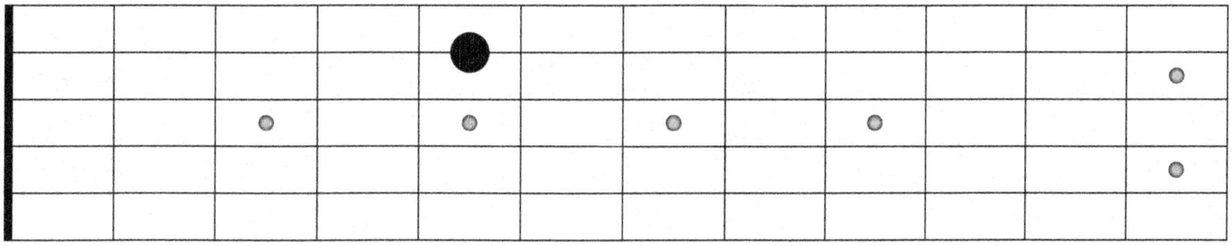

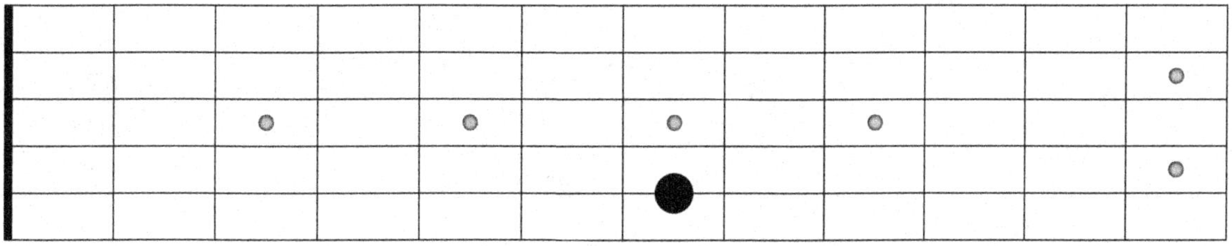

E

E

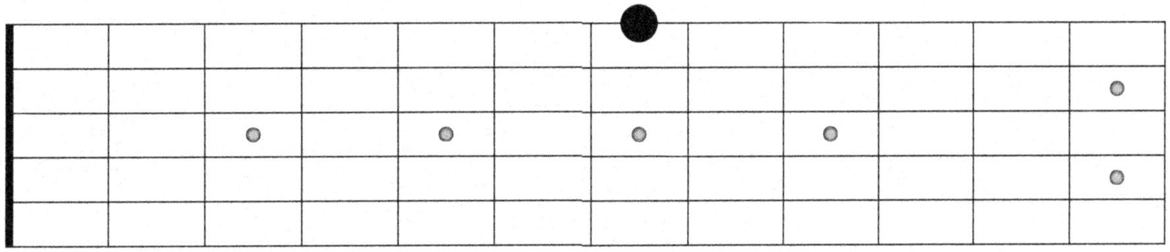

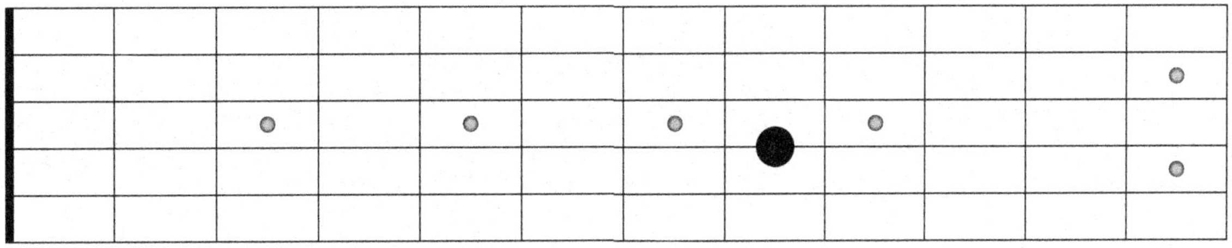

B

A#

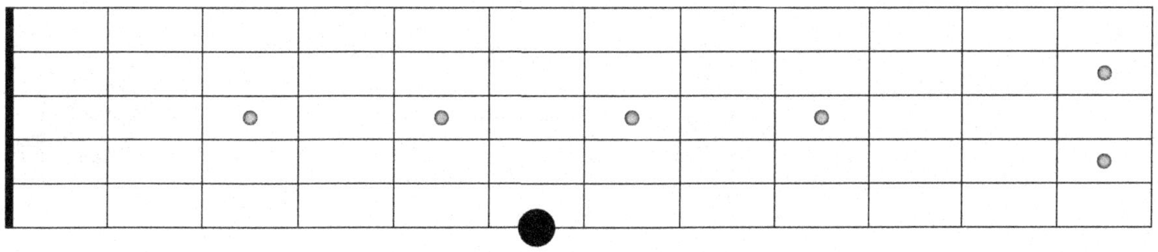

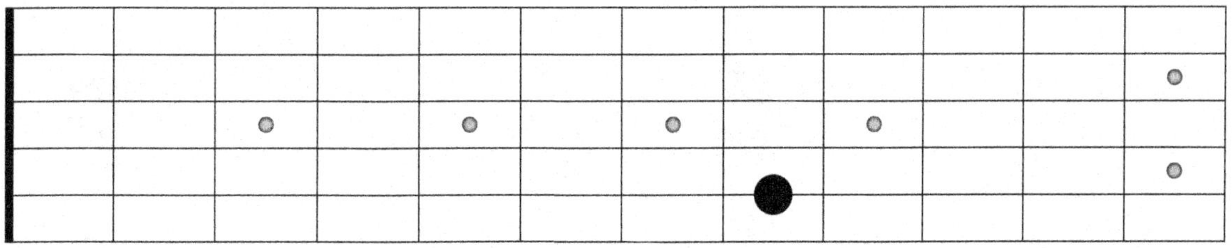

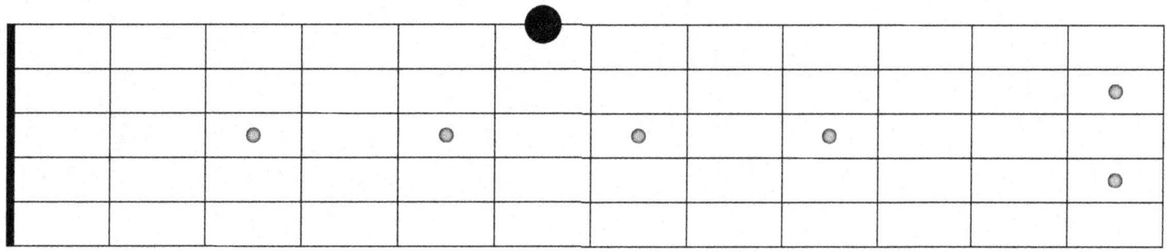

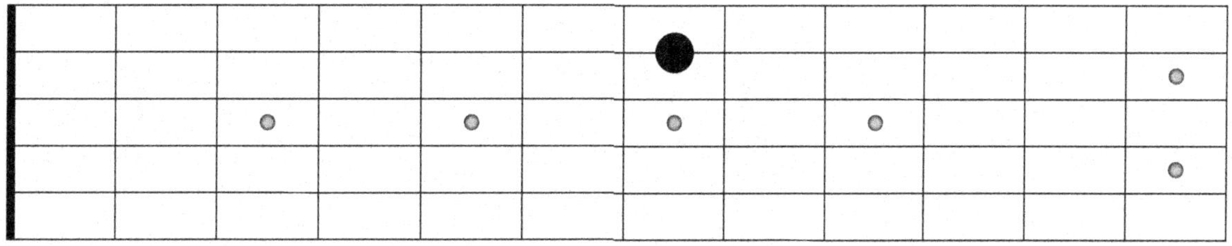

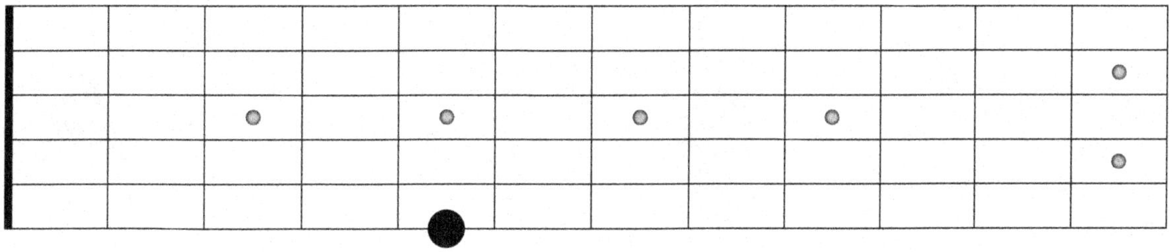

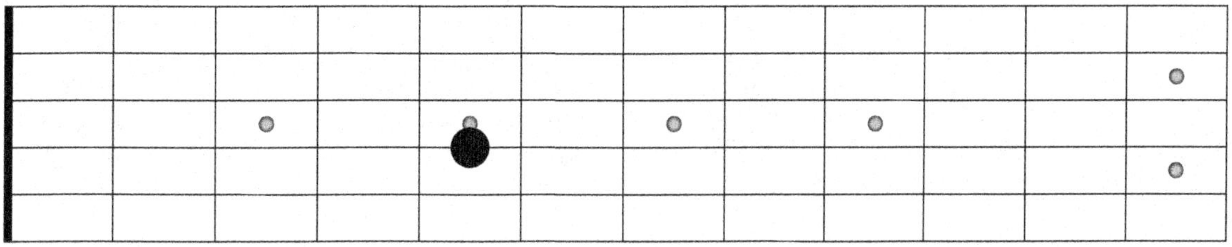

A

G

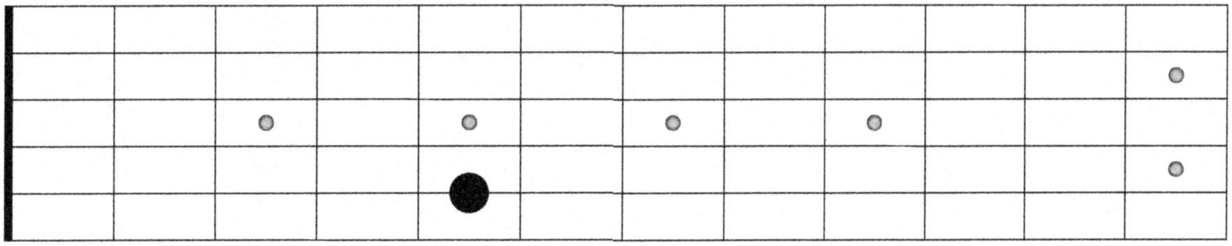

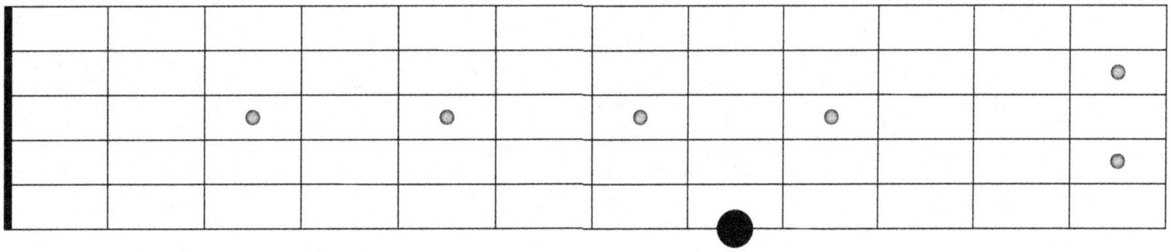

D

C

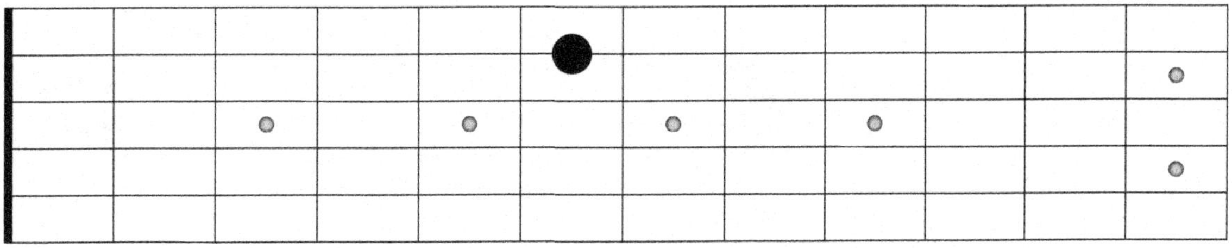

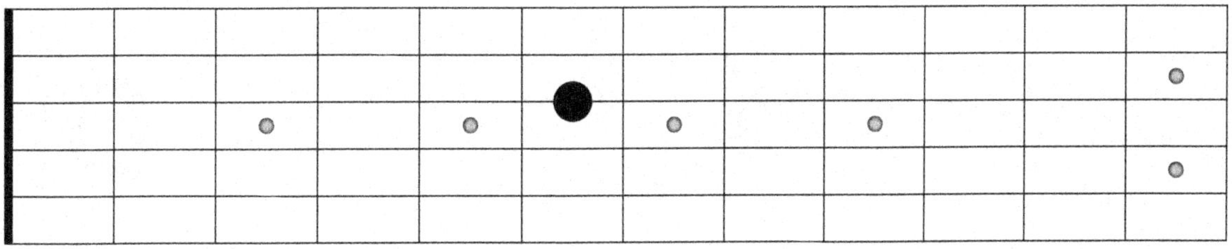

F

D♭

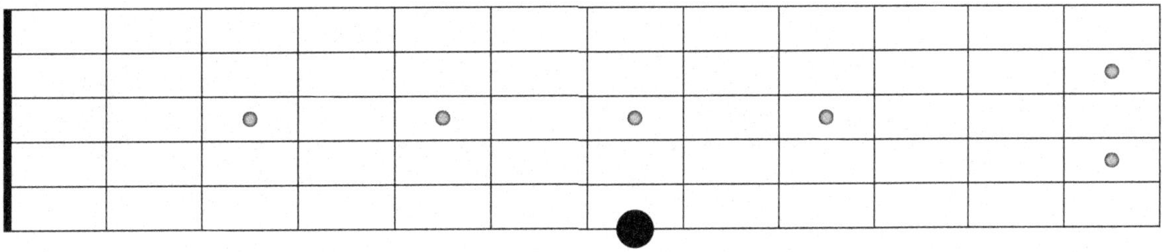

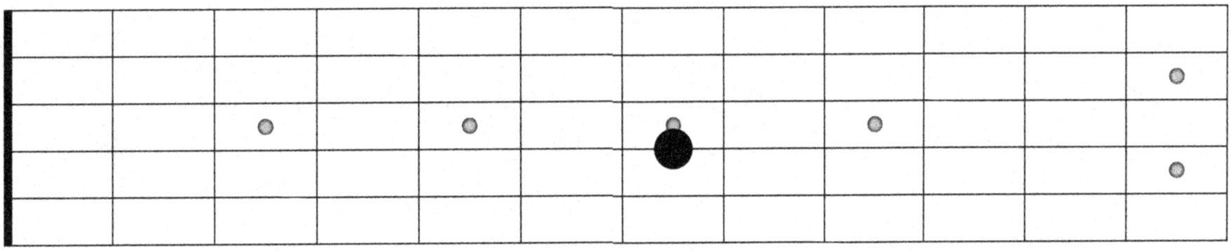

B

A

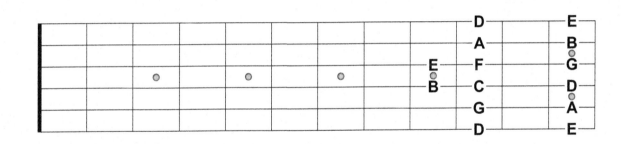

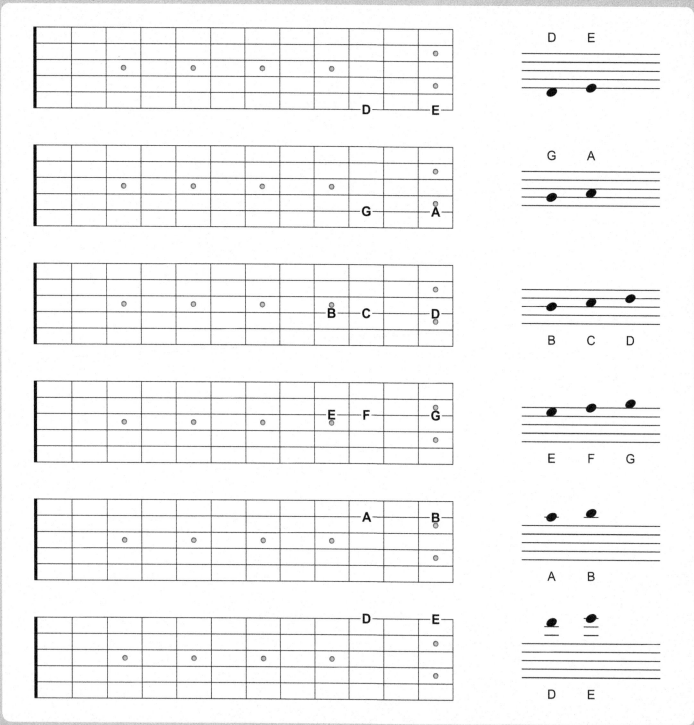

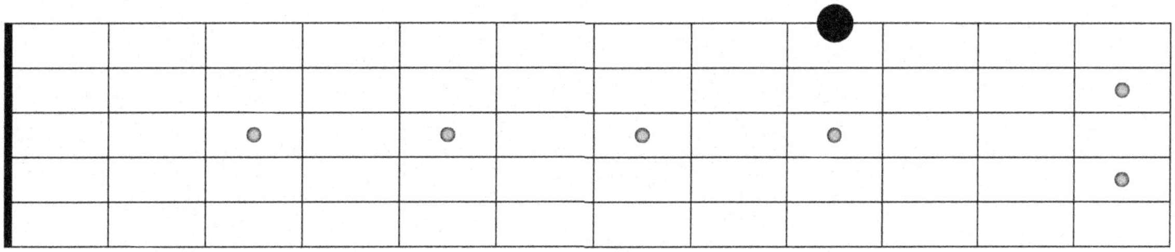

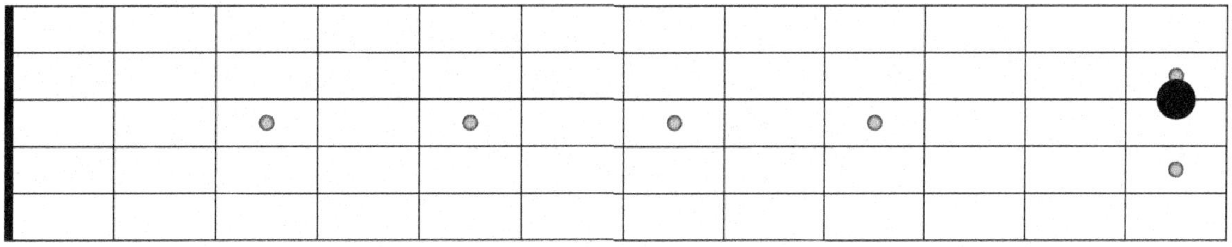

C#

G

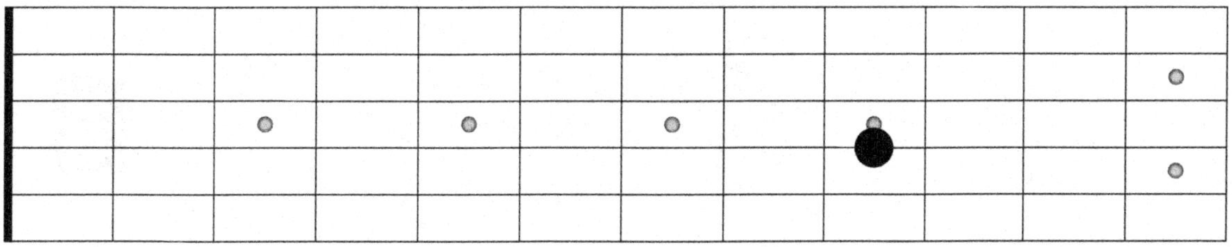

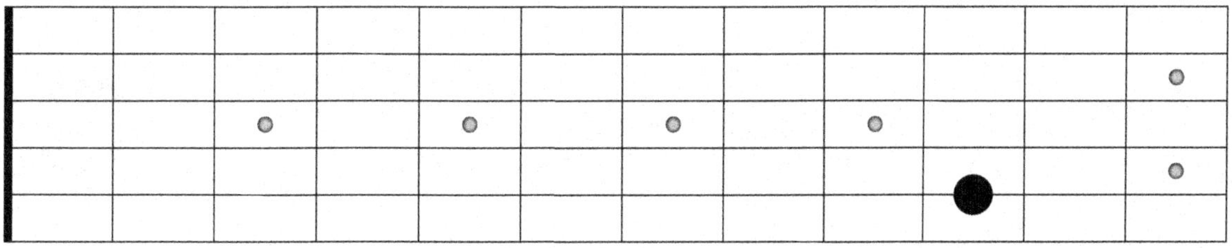

B

G

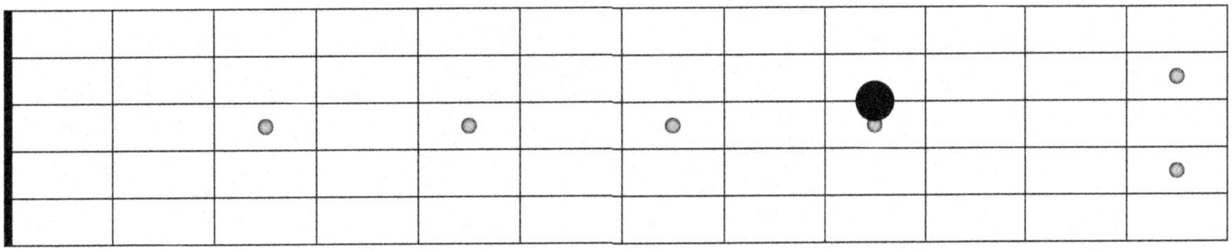

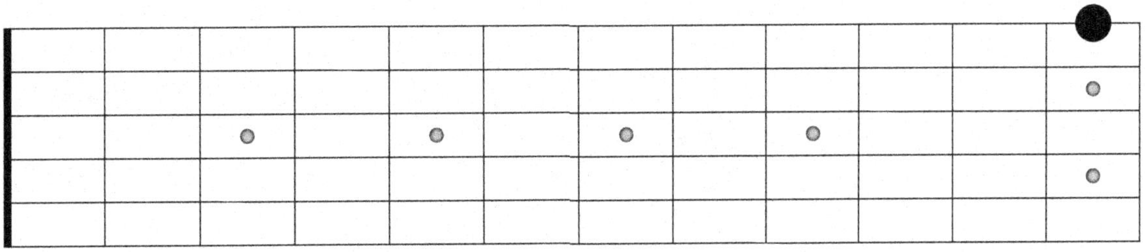

E

E

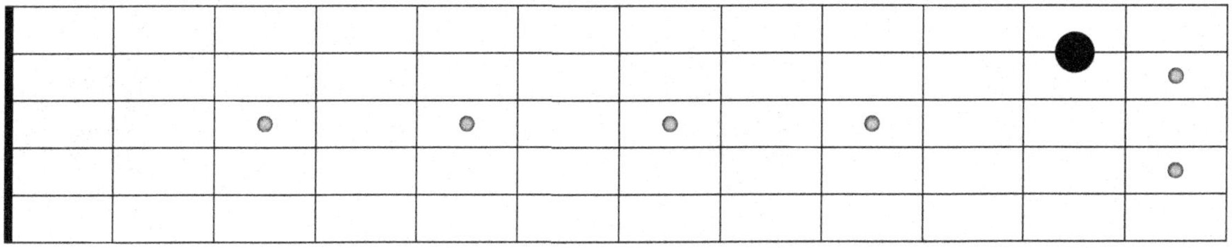

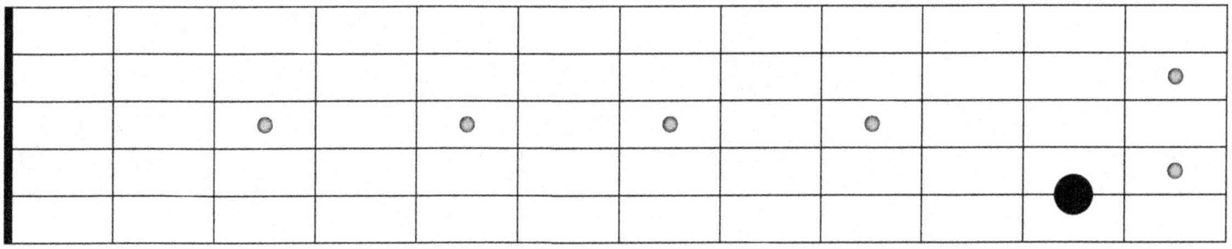

B♭

A♭

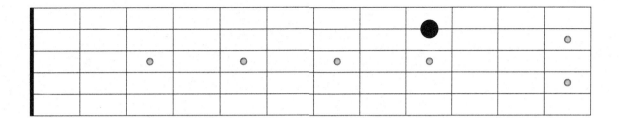

E

A♭

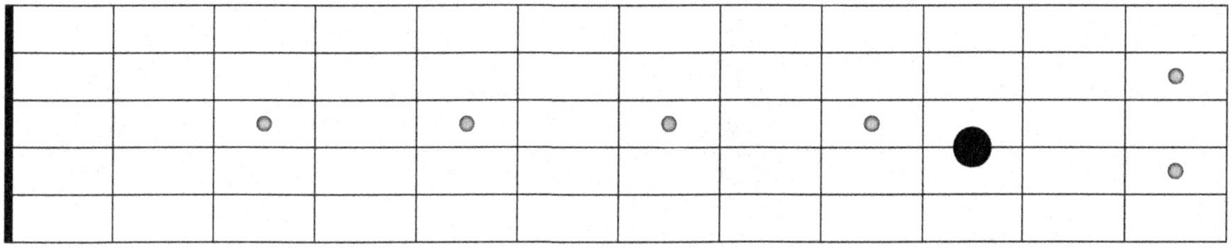

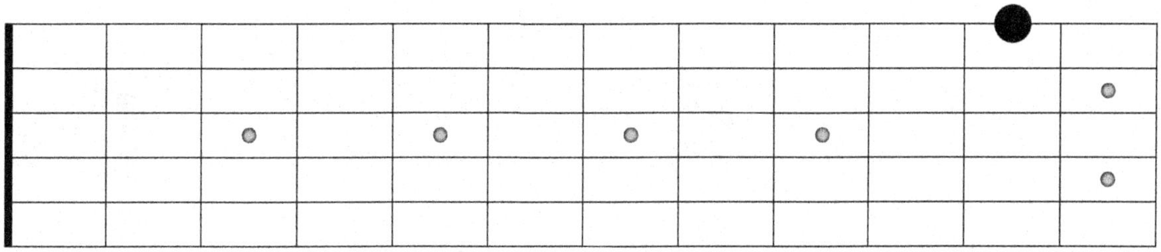

C

D♯

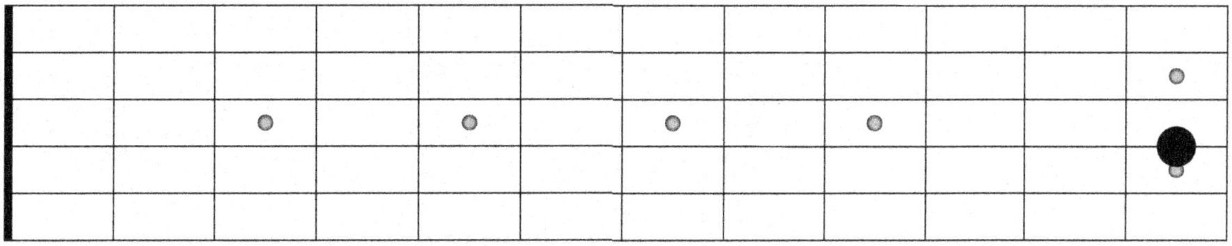

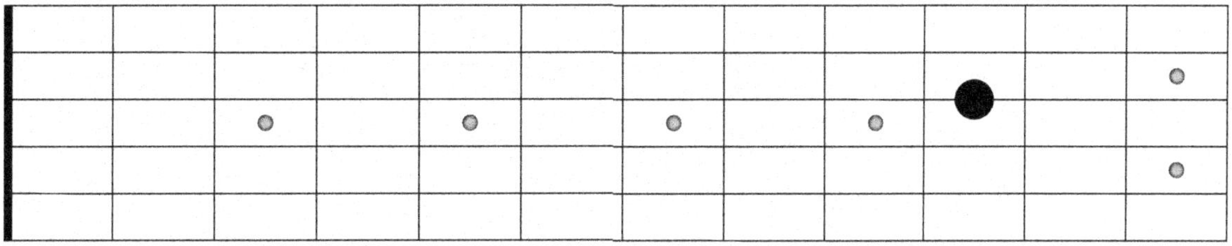

D

F

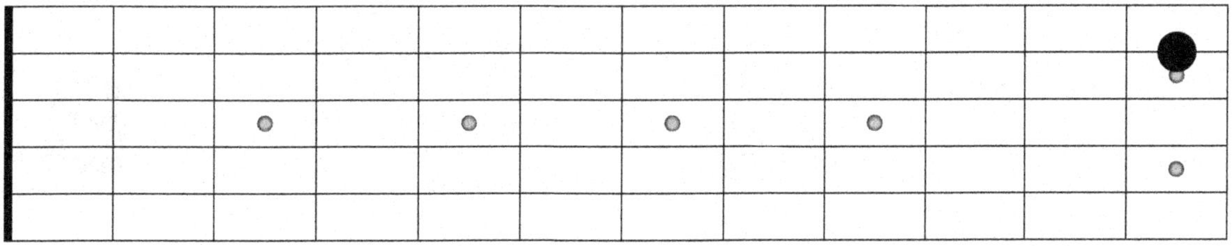

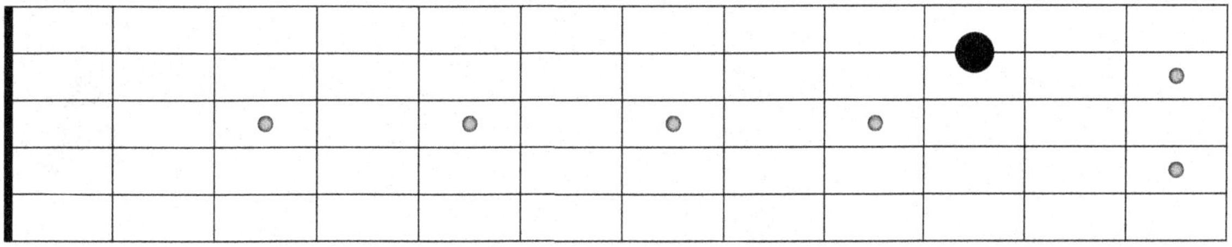

B

A

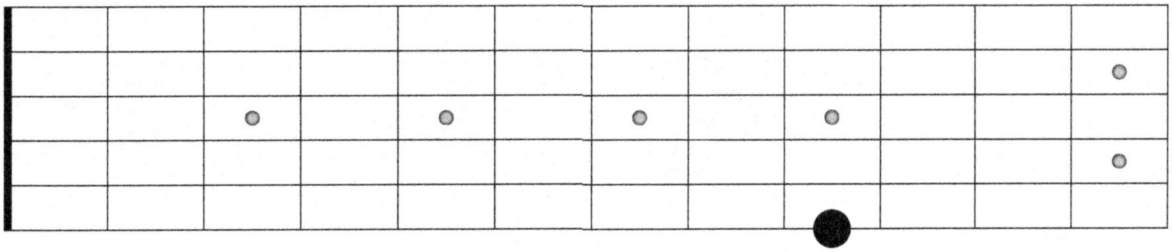

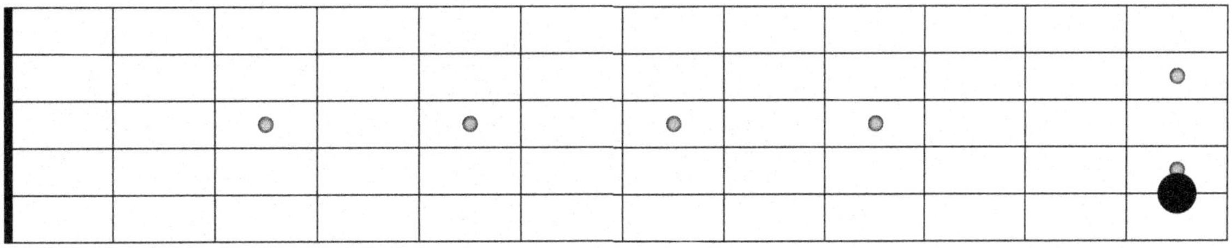

D♭

A

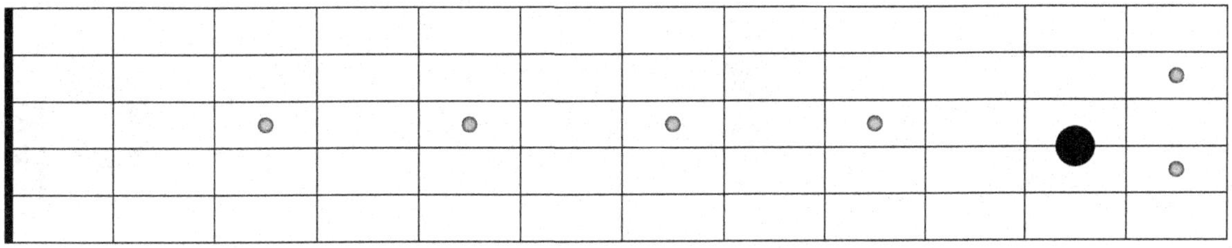

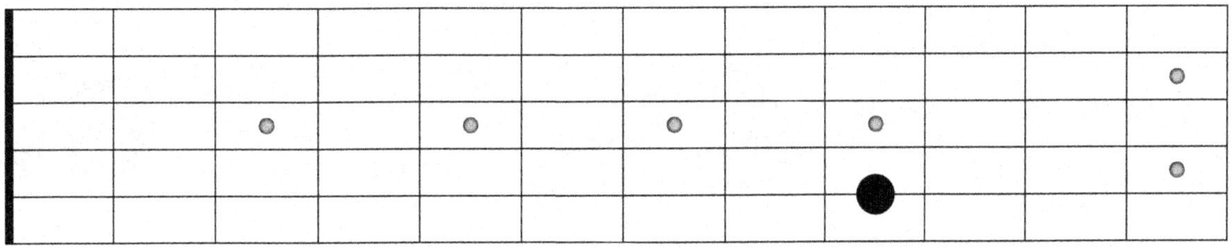

C♯

G♭

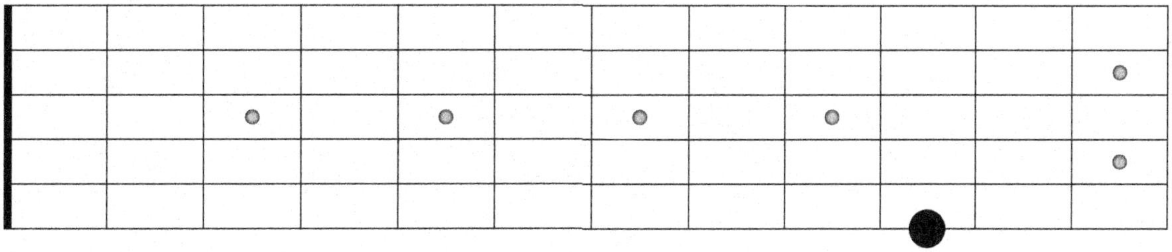

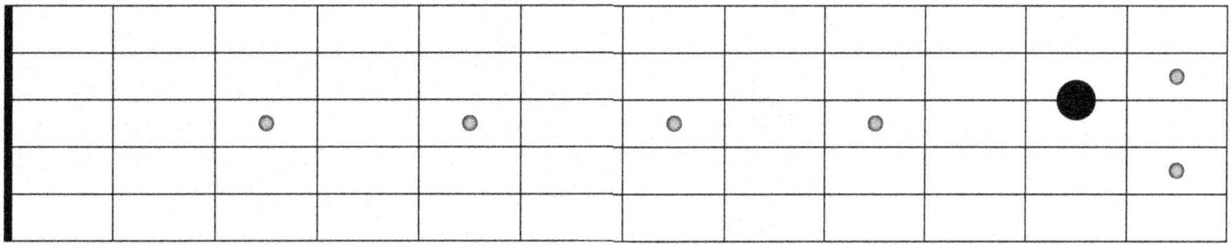

D

G♭

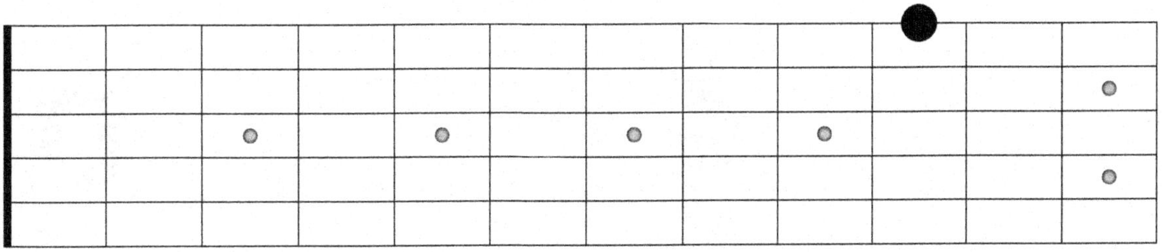

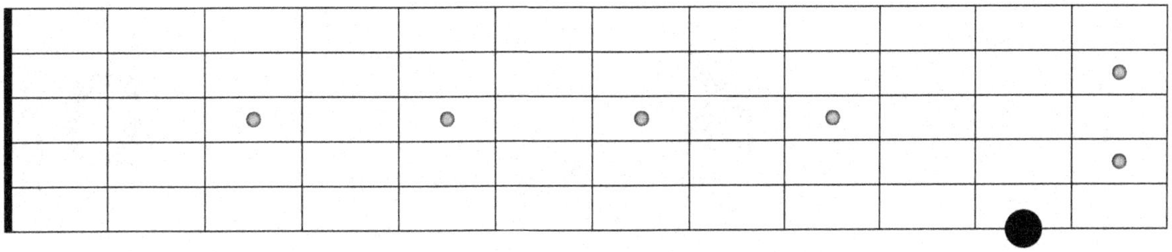

D

D♯

Pêle-Mêle WORKS

[**pelemeleworks.**com]

- *MUSIC PAPER*, the manuscript paper series.
  a range of blank manuscript paper designs for guitar and other instruments,
  available in pocketbook and notebook formats.

  pelemeleworks.com

- *CHEATSHEET Music*, the music cheatsheet series.
  a series of practical cheatsheets on key music topics for the musician,
  teacher, and student.

  cheatsheetmusic.com

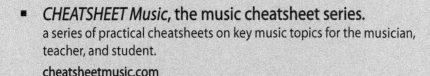

- *INTERVALLIC FRETBOARD – Towards Improvising on the Guitar.*
  a thought-provoking book on fretboard visualisation, using intervals to
  understand its geometric properties and navigate its layout.

  intervallicfretboard.com

- *GUITAR FINGERS – Essential Technique in Pictures.*
  an in-depth tutorial on left hand and right hand technique for guitar,
  through pictures and short exercises.

  pelemeleworks.com

- *GUITAR NOTE FINDER.*
  a handy aid to help memorise the notes on the fretboard and map them to
  the music staff.

  pelemeleworks.com

CPSIA information can be obtained
at www.ICGtesting.com
Printed in the USA
BVOW04s0859050118
504345BV00008B/123/P